AI in Hospitality

Innovative Solutions for Travel and Tourism

Table of Contents

Chapter 1. Introduction

Welcome to a cutting-edge exploration of "AI in Hospitality: Innovative Solutions for Travel and Tourism"! Our special report intertwines real-world applications of artificial intelligence with the ever-evolving landscape of the hospitality industry. In a language that is both accessible and engaging, we unpack how AI-driven solutions are influencing every touchpoint from personalized amenities to predictive hotel room pricing. This comprehensive review beckons the curious, the profession-enthusiasts, and technophiles alike. By the end, you'll not only understand the scale of innovation at play but also be inspired by the transformative power of technological advancements in shaping the way we experience travel and tourism. Immerse yourself in this eye-opening journey, and you'll soon realize why this special report is a must-have guide for navigating the future of hospitality!

Chapter 2. Navigating the AI Landscape in Hospitality

Artificial Intelligence (AI), once the realm of science fiction, has firmly rooted itself into our everyday lives and industries, including hospitality. The way we travel, make bookings, and experience hotels is changing rapidly due to the evolution of AI technologies.

2.1. The Inception of AI in Hospitality

AI is not an entirely new concept in hospitality, though its capabilities have expanded exponentially in recent years. Since the advent of the Internet, hospitality companies have used digital platforms to facilitate reservations and communicate with customers. The difference now is that AI turns these interactions into valuable data which, when properly analyzed and applied, can have a transformative effect on operations, customer relationships, and profitability.

The crossover between AI and hospitality is a relatively recent development, but its impact has already been profound. Early efforts at integrating these technologies focused on improving operations and efficiencies. For instance, using an Interactive Voice Assistant (IVA) like Alexa to handle routine tasks, like turning on lights or ordering room service, frees up front desk staff and housekeeping.

2.2. AI-driven Personalization: The New Standard

Personalized services and experiences play a critical role in the hospitality industry. AI technology enables these personalized experiences by using data from customer interactions to learn preferences and behaviors, thereby making more accurate predictions about what a customer might want or need.

For example, AI systems can analyze booking data and customer feedback to identify patterns and trends. If a regular customer always books a room with a sea view, the system could automatically present this option first during the booking process. Similarly, if a guest often orders room service from a particular restaurant, AI can recommend similar restaurants in the area, creating a more personalized experience for the guest.

2.3. Chatbots: The 24/7 Customer Support

Chatbots, a widely adopted AI technology, have seen pronounced use in hospitality. These AI-powered virtual assistants offer 24/7 support handling frequently asked questions, making reservations, processing payments, and more. Accustomed to on-demand service, the modern customer greatly appreciates the fast response times and round-the-clock accessibility provided by chatbots. They offer both a cost-effective way for hospitality businesses to provide consistent customer service and an innovative solution to enhancing the customer experience.

2.4. AI and Revenue Management

AI has revolutionized revenue management in hospitality. Historically, setting room rates was a complex task involving analysis of booking trends, competitors' rates, local events, and more. Today, AI can do this job with increased accuracy and efficiency.

AI algorithms can process large amounts of data, allowing them to forecast future demand with remarkable precision. This ability to anticipate future booking trends and adjust prices accordingly has allowed for smarter, more fluid pricing strategies that respond to market dynamics in real time.

2.5. Transforming the Guest Experience: AI Concierge Services

One of the most noted advancements in hospitality AI is the introduction of AI concierge services. These virtual concierges, either in the form of mobile apps or smart devices in hotel rooms, use AI to learn from each guest interaction, offering personalized service and improving recommendations over time.

The guest's comfort, convenience, and personalized experience are at the forefront of these technologies. Whether it's offering dining recommendations, booking tickets, arranging transportation, or suggesting itineraries, these AI-powered concierge services endow the guest with a highly customized experience.

In conclusion, AI's myriad tools and technologies are revolutionizing the hospitality industry. They facilitate operational efficiency, streamline communications, enhance revenue management, and most importantly, craft personalized guest experiences that are the cornerstone of outstanding hospitality. As AI becomes more sophisticated, we can expect further innovative applications that will continue to transform the hospitality landscape. Whether a seasoned industry insider or a tech-savvy traveler, understanding how AI is shaping this industry will likely be integral to navigating its future.

Chapter 3. AI-Powered Personalization: Revolutionizing the Guest Experience

Personalization is no longer a mere buzzword in the hospitality industry – it has become a compelling force that is reshaping the way businesses operate. Artificial Intelligence (AI) plays a pivotal role in this metamorphosis, enabling an unparalleled level of customization that enriches every guest's experience. Let's delve into this fascinating domain and see how AI-powered personalization revolutionizes the guest experience in the hospitality sector.

3.1. Unearthing the Potential of AI in Personalization

Personalization with the muscle power of artificial intelligence is far more potent than traditional methods. It involves understanding customer behaviour and predicting their preferences using AI. In many ways, AI-powered personalization directly influences a hotel's ability to attract, satisfy, and retain customers.

AI predicts guest preferences by analyzing past behavioural patterns, social media inputs, customer feedback, and a plethora of other personal and impersonal data sources. Machine Learning (ML), a pivotal branch of AI, allows the system to learn and adapt, becoming more accurate in its predictions over time.

AI-powered personalization transcends the confines of basic amenities. It manifests itself in various ways - from tailoring the room temperature to a person's liking, suggesting local attractions based on preferences, to customizing meal preferences.

3.2. AI-Powered Amenities – A Pathway to Luxury and Comfort

The AI prowess in personalizing amenities amplifies the sense of luxury and comfort a guest experiences. Imagine walking into a hotel room that matches your home's temperature preferences or where the television springs alive with your favorite channel. AI is not just about enhancing luxuries; it is about creating a sense of home away from home.

Internet of Things (IoT) devices armed with AI capabilities can assimilate guest preferences, allowing hoteliers to customize everything – from lighting and temperature to televisions and music systems. AI-layered Smart mirrors or AI-based voice assistants can further decipher a guest's needs, making their stay more luxurious and comfortable.

3.3. Tasting Success with AI-Driven Food and Beverage Enhancements

AI's influence extends to the food and beverage sector of hospitality where it refines the gastronomical experience of the guests. By analyzing dietary needs, allergy information, and past food orders, AI can suggest menu items, aiding guests in discovering new delicacies and helping hotels upsell their offerings.

Intelligent recommendation engines powered by AI and ML algorithms can go a step further, offering wine pairing suggestions or recommending a cocktail based on the guest's previous choices. Moreover, these AI systems can identify trending food and beverage preferences, helping hotels to optimize their menus for maximum appeal and revenue.

3.4. Facilitating Seamless Experiences with AI in Operations

AI affects not just the fringes of the guest experience but the core operational aspects as well. AI aids in streamlining hotel operations, ensuring that every guest's stay is hassle-free – from check-in to check-out.

AI can manage room assignments based on guest preferences, such as type of room, view preferences, or a particular floor or wing. An AI-based property management system can optimize hotel operations, assisting in managing pace of bookings, and offering dynamic pricing based on demand and supply, creating an advantageous situation for both hoteliers and guests.

3.5. AI at the Front Desk – A New Era Of Customer Interaction

AI reshapes the way hotels interact with their guests. AI-powered chatbots and voice assistants answer queries, handle complaints, and assist with bookings 24/7, ensuring an immediate response to guest needs.

Furthermore, facial recognition technology helps expedite and personalize the check-in process; guests can be greeted by their names, a delightful personal touch that enhances customer satisfaction. The technology also increases security by ensuring only registered guests access certain facilities.

3.6. The After-hour Appeal – AI-Powered Entertainment and Local Exploration

Beyond in-hotel offerings, AI provides tourism and local exploration suggestions based on a guest's interests and preferences. Be it a wine connoisseur wanting to explore local vineyards, a nature lover keen to hike local trails, or a history buff wanting to visit nearby museums, AI platforms can propose personalized itineraries.

The blend of AI in hospitality creates a celebration of personal touchpoints, creating experiences that resonate with each guest by catering to their unique taste and preference. It orchestrates a symphony of personalized experiences that leaves guests truly delighted, making their stay not just comfortable but truly memorable.

Through these developments, AI-powered personalization is bringing a revolution in the hospitality industry, invigorating the landscape with promise and potential. As further advancements unfold, the day when AI personalized experiences become a 'standard' offering rather than a 'luxury' isn't too far off. As we continue to embrace AI's transformative power, personalization in hospitality is poised to reach new heights, creating an era marked by a profound allegiance to individuality and customer delight.

Chapter 4. Predictive Analytics: Optimizing Pricing and Occupancy Rates

AI has inundated every sphere of the hospitality industry, including one of the most critical dimensions - pricing and occupancy. Leveraging the power of predictive analytics, hotels can now implement dynamic pricing strategies and optimize their occupancy rates.

4.1. The New Wave of Dynamic Pricing

Dynamic pricing is not a new concept in the hospitality field. Hotels have been riding the wave of fluctuating prices for decades to account for seasonal swings, booking timelines, and occupancy rates. Yet, AI introduces a transformative capacity for further enhancing these strategies, allowing for precise, perhaps near-perfect, price modulation.

Traditional models primarily relied on a rudimentary set of parameters, such as fixed seasonal changes, holidays, and weekends. While these factors are still essential, AI and machine learning have widened this spectrum, broaching previously unattainable accuracy by considering an extensive range of factors to determine pricing suggestions to maximize revenue.

Factors such as weather forecasts, local events, customer booking behaviors, competitive pricing, historical booking trends, and even social media sentiment are evaluated in real-time, which underpins the refined facet of AI-based dynamic pricing strategies. With its data-crunching abilities, AI can make sense of this labyrinth of data, remarkably downplaying human biases and potential mistakes.

4.2. Real-Time Revenue Management

AI-powered predictive analytics are extending their influence over revenue management, largely relied on for making critical pricing decisions. Real-time data from various sources is readily available thanks to technology advancement, making room for a comprehensive and dynamic revenue management strategy.

AI's additional selling point here is its capacity to work with Big Data. Handling mass-scale data sets has been a persistent complication for industries, let alone applying this data for decision-making. With cutting-edge machine learning algorithms, AI can sift through voluminous data, drawing out relevant trends and patterns.

In revenue management, this capability allows for continuous forecast adjustments and ideal pricing strategies. Hotels can leverage AI, thence, to ensure optimal room rates at any given point while considering factors previously outside their immediate consideration, such as economic indicators and flight booking trends.

4.3. AI in Demand Forecasting

Apprehending future demand is another considerable challenge hotels face; faltering here could mean either lost revenue due to overpricing or an unchecked loss from underpricing. Machine learning, a subset of AI, comes to play here fruitfully, enabling more accurate demand forecasting.

Machine learning, through its neural networks and deep learning models, can learn and adapt from previous booking data. The more data it has access to, the more accurate its predictions can become. Over time, ML can significantly improve a hotel's demand forecasting, supporting timely and relevant pricing changes.

Apart from historical booking data, ML also considers irregularities such as local events, sudden weather changes, or natural disasters that might influence demand. By capturing these irregularities in its algorithm, ML can provide a preventive measure for unforeseen circumstances. The foresight offered by such analytics can help hotels better manage their resources and staffing requirements, enhancing their overall service levels.

4.4. Case Study: MARi, An AI-Powered Solution

An illustration of AI's effect in hotel pricing and occupancy optimization is MARi, an AI solution by P3 Hotels. By integrating various external data points such as competitor rates, guest reviews, events, and flight data, combined with the hotel's own booking pace, MARi gives hoteliers real-time pricing and inventory recommendations.

MARi employs machine learning to make predictions on booking behavior based on historical data. It takes into account different booking types like group, corporate, or individual bookings. Based on the data, MARi updates its inventory and room rate predictions daily, helping hotels optimize revenue and better meet guest expectations.

4.5. Conclusion: The Edge Provided by AI and Predictive Analytics

Embracing AI and predictive analytics in price and occupancy optimization opens up a broad vista of opportunities for hotels striving for market competitiveness. By capitalizing on these predictive capabilities, businesses can foresee and respond to various market dynamics more effectively, which is integral in the fluid world of hospitality.

Although the utilization of AI and machine learning still rests in its infancy, the potential associated with this technology harbors great potential for bringing a paradigm shift in the hospitality industry's pricing and occupancy practices. It promises to usher in a transformative era of accuracy, efficiency, and profitability that can help shape a more sustainable and balanced industry, justifying AI's impressive standing in the hospitality horizon.

Chapter 5. Virtual Concierges: The Future of Guest Services

Stepping into a hotel lobby, the first person encountered by a guest is usually the concierge. They are the meeting point of guest services, the key handlers of queries, requests, and concerns. But this cornerstone of hospitality is transitioning from a solely human role to potentially being shouldered by artificial intelligence. Introducing the concept of virtual concierges; a seamless blend of technology and service.

5.1. The Birth of Virtual Concierges

Virtual concierges are automated systems powered by artificial intelligence. They massage a series of coded instructions into warm, proactive, and responsive service experiences. They draw on historical data, real-time updates, and AI algorithms to address a broad spectrum of guest queries and demands. From booking services to providing suggestions for local attractions, these AI-powered assistants are redefining the limits of customer service in the hospitality industry.

The motivation for virtual concierges arose from the sector's ultimate mission: to deliver personalized, top-tier service to every guest. As technology continued to breakthrough barriers, it created a platform where instant response and around-the-clock availability were no longer pipe dreams, but operational norms. With AI taking the reins, hoteliers are finding more efficient ways to meet customer expectations.

5.2. Technological Underpinnings of Virtual Concierges

Most virtual concierges are built on Natural Language Processing (NLP) units: a branch of AI that deals with the interaction between computers and human language. Using NLP, the AI analyses text inputs and audio commands, extracting relevant information and formulating appropriate responses.

Some applications are voice-activated and interact through verbal communication, much like Google Assistant, Siri, or Amazon's Alexa. For instance, guests can ask these virtual concierges for weather updates, restaurant recommendations, or even trivia facts. Guided by Machine Learning (ML) algorithms, these AI entities improve their answers over time, incorporating feedback and expanding their knowledge base with each interaction.

Beyond voice recognition, advances in sensor technology and Internet of Things (IoT) devices have expanded the functionality of virtual concierges. They can now control room temperature, lighting, and even entertainment units, thereby offering a highly personalized and interactive guest experience.

5.3. The Integration Challenge: A Two-Pronged Approach

Integrating AI into the hospitality system is a two-pronged challenge: technical infrastructure and user experience. The first involves equipping entire properties with the necessary hardware. A hotel needs adequate Wi-Fi coverage, cutting-edge servers, IoT-enabled devices, and voice-activated assistants. The second prong is ensuring seamless user experience. This requires easy-to-use interfaces, well-planned responses to common queries, and troubleshooting guides for·the inevitable technological hitches.

5.4. Business Advantages of Virtual Concierges

Virtual concierges are quickly becoming game-changers in the hospitality sector. By offering 24/7 service, these AI-mediated assistants are redefining the limits of customer service. Their instant response capability improves customer satisfaction, while their constant availability caters to the around-the-clock needs of guests from different time zones.

They also optimize resources by executing routine tasks, thereby freeing up human staff for more sophisticated guest requests. This may lead to more personalized service, operational efficiency, and reduced running costs.

For the industry, virtual concierges offer unparalleled data analytics capabilities. They can track user preferences, detect patterns, and generate reports, thus providing valuable customer insight. Hoteliers can use this data to inform decision-making, refine services, and create targeted marketing.

5.5. Creating Engaging and Human-like Interactions

Looking ahead, the challenge for the industry is to strike a balance: maximizing efficiency and personalization while maintaining the human touch that is central to hospitality. Ensuring the virtual concierge can engage in more than sterile responses will be key. Training these AI systems to understand emotion, pick up on subtle cues, and respond with empathy could be the breakthrough calling.

5.6. The Road Ahead

While the road to full integration of AI into the hospitality sector is still under construction, there's no denying that virtual concierges are at the heart of this revolution. Certain small- and large-scale hotels have already begun to embrace this with gusto and are reaping rewards.

The journey towards implementing these cutting-edge AI technologies is admittedly a challenging one. It requires substantial investment in infrastructure, an appetite for continual learning and adaptation, and most critically, a willingness to re-imagine the service experience. However, the potential benefits – invigorated operational efficiency, a highly personalized guest experience, and enriched business insights – make it a worthwhile pursuit.

As we move forward, let's remember: the future of hospitality revolves around human-centered innovation. The adoption of AI and virtual concierges is not about replacing humans but augmenting their abilities. It's about taking service levels to heights unimagined and re-defining the future of guest services. After all, hospitality is a blend of service and innovation and its future lies at the intersection of these two pathways.

Chapter 6. Machine Learning and Its Impact on Travel Recommendations

Machine Learning (ML) has been a game-changer for numerous industries, and it is having a profound impact within the realm of travel and tourism as well. Predicated on the algorithms that empower computers to learn from and act on data, ML is shaping the dynamic landscape of travel recommendations, powering more individualization, and improving efficiency in unprecedented ways.

6.1. The Evolution of Machine Learning: A Brief Overview

Machine Learning is a branch of artificial intelligence that provides systems the ability to learn and improve from experience without being explicitly programmed. This technology thrives on patterns and trends in data, learning progressively to accomplish tasks and make decisions that endow machines with near-human intelligence. ML models leverage large streams of data and continually adapt and learn from them, ensuring up-to-date responsiveness to a user's needs or a change in the environment.

Over the years, machine learning transitioned from being a purely academical interest to powering billions of real-world applications. From recognition systems used by social media companies to prove their users' identity, to prediction models that enable personal financial advice, machine learning is already weaved into the fabric of our everyday lives.

6.2. Machine Learning in the Hospitality and Travel Industry

The hospitality and travel industry thrives on providing memorable experiences, and Machine Learning has shifted the paradigm on how these experiences are formulated. From flight booking platforms, hotel chains, and vacation recommendation services, the efficacy of services rendered has remarkably improved owing to ML.

Traditionally, travel recommendations were primarily based on broad parameters like location, dates, and budgets. However, in this era of hyper-personalized experiences, such broad suggestions are no longer sufficient. Customers seek experiences tailored to their specific preferences, needs, and desires. It is here that machine learning provides a transformative solution.

6.3. Data-driven Personalization: Machine Learning democratizing Travel Recommendations

Machine learning utilizes historic data to intuit the preferences of a customer. A ML-driven system can analyze past booking trends, activity preferences, behavioral patterns on the website, or application, to offer personally tailored recommendations. The beneficial offshoot of this approach is a higher conversion rate as the customers find the suggestions more in line with their expectations.

For instance, if a user habitually books seaside hotels and engages with articles related to aquatic adventure sports, the machine learning algorithm will direct such hotels and activities the next time this user is looking to plan a vacation.

Over time, the system becomes better at understanding user

inclinations, offering more target-specific and personalized travel recommendations. What's more, is that this level of precision extends to other aspects of travel planning like transport modes, meal preferences, and places of interest.

6.4. Predictive Analytics: Enhancing Customer Service and Revenue Management

Predictive analytics, a key application of machine learning, is proving instrumental in enhancing revenue management and customer service in travel and tourism. Using historical data and customer behavior trends, predictive models forecast customer response, market developments, and revenue growth.

Hotels, for example, can use predictive analytics to adjust prices in real-time based on factors like demand, competitor pricing, and local events. Such dynamic pricing not only boosts revenue but also improves room occupancy rates.

Predictive analytics can also play a crucial role in enhancing customer service. By analyzing data on customer satisfaction and feedback, predictive models can flag potential issues that may affect customer experience and provide actionable insights to address them proactively.

6.5. Machine Learning: Driving Efficiency and Sustainability

Machine Learning can play a pivotal role in driving efficiency and sustainability efforts in the travel industry. Stochastic problems like traffic predictions, optimal routing, and energy usage could be solved more accurately and faster using ML algorithms. This could translate to significant cost savings, improve efficiency, and contribute to sustainable practices.

For instance, airlines can use ML to optimize routes based on weather patterns and air traffic, leading to fuel savings and reduce carbon emissions. Similarly, hotels can use machine learning to optimize energy usage based on occupancy and time of day.

6.6. The Road Ahead: Challenges and Opportunities

As with any groundbreaking technology, machine learning does not come without its challenges. As it relies on data, ensuring its privacy, security and ethical use is of utmost importance. Furthermore, the algorithms need to be trained in a way that they are not biased, making the recommendations fair and equitable.

Despite some hurdles, the road ahead for ML in the hospitality and travel industry is undoubtedly promising. As machine learning models are further refined and more industry-tailored solutions are developed, we will see an acceleration in the adoption of this technology. It will not only transform interactions and experiences but also render a more efficient, customer-centric, and sustainable travel and tourism industry.

Through this shift towards a more personalized, insightful, and eco-conscious service, Machine Learning is revolutionizing the scope of travel recommendations, offering an inspiring glimpse into the future of the hospitality and travel industry as a whole, driven by data-driven decisions and intuitive experiences.

Chapter 7. Robotic Process Automation in Hotel Operations

Artificial Intelligence (AI) is weaving its transformative spell across the industrial landscape, and the hospitality sector is no exception. One AI-driven technology significantly impacting this sector is Robotic Process Automation (RPA), a game-changing innovation aimed at optimizing various facets of hotel operations. While some might view this trend with caution, industry leaders have embraced RPA as a pathway to enhanced efficiency, reduced costs, and improved guest experiences.

7.1. Unlocking Efficiency with RPA

The manual data entry, file management, and routine tasks traditionally involved in hotel operations can be time-consuming, inefficient, and prone to error. Cue RPA. This technology automates these repetitive tasks, granting employees more creative freedom and strategic responsibilities. Automations can range from check-in and check-out procedures, managing guest data, processing payments, to scheduling room cleaning. The results? Minimized human errors, efficient use of resources, and fast-passed work processes— with guest satisfaction as the added cherry on top.

7.2. Cost-saving Potential of RPA

In the world of hotel management, RPA has the capacity to trim excess costs away significantly. The technology's capability to operate round-the-clock without pause brings substantial cost reductions to the table. For instance, automating back-office operations with RPA eliminates the need for hiring additional staff, reducing labour costs.

Additionally, the technology's accuracy and consistency minimize costly error rates typically associated with manual operations. As RPA systems can be adjusted to accommodate varying workload levels, hotels can employ a flexible cost structure, scaling their operations depending on their needs.

7.3. RPA's Role in Improving Customer Experience

As the shift from product-focused to customer-centric service intensifies, a hotel's ability to provide a personalized, seamless, and exceptional guest experience becomes paramount. Thanks to RPA, hotels can now offer just that— customizable experiences tailored to individual preferences. By automating tasks and processes, employees are freed up to engage with customers on a personal level. Automated booking systems can offer room preferences based on past guest data, recommend additional amenities or special offers, and even schedule facilities usage to avoid crowding. Similarly, automated guest data collection and management can help hotels anticipate and cater to customer needs, providing a more personalized and satisfying stay.

7.4. The Role of RPA in Data Management and Analysis

In the vast sea of data that hotels handle daily, RPA serves as a lighthouse, effectively sorting and managing this data. From organizing booking information to compiling structured reports, RPA simplifies tedious data processes, letting hotel executives leverage insights easily. The technology also assists in predictive analysis, helping hotels forecast trends: think optimal pricing, future bookings, or seasonal variations. By providing an informed base for decisions, RPA helps hotels stay competitive and profitable.

7.5. Integrating RPA— Challenges and Potential Solutions

Though the promise of RPA is monumental, the practical integration of this technology in hotel operations isn't without its hurdles. From uncertainty about adoption costs, resistance to change among staff, to concerns about technical glitches, these challenges are real. Yet, they can be overcome. Developing a structured implementation plan, building employee awareness and buy-in, and providing appropriate training could smoothen these road bumps. Additionally, partnering with a skilled RPA provider that understands the specific needs and nuances of the hotel industry can ensure a productive integration.

In summary, RPA is not a far-off concept in hotel operations; rather, it is very much a part of the sector's current landscape. While the challenges of implementing this technology may be sizeable, the potential for enhanced efficiency, cost savings, and superior customer service that RPA brings is undeniably attractive. As the hospitality industry continues to evolve, Robotic Process Automation could soon be the gold standard in hotel management, setting the stage for an AI-powered era of service. As readers, we can take heart from the boundless potential RPA holds and look forward to witnessing its transformative power in the hospitality universe.

Chapter 8. AI's Role in Driving Sustainable Practices in the Tourism Industry

AI has established resonance within the domains of finance, healthcare, manufacturing and now, we're observing its burgeoning impact in the hospitality industry. Among the many transformations imparted, the most distinctive is driving sustainability - a concern steadily gathering prominence amidst the ongoing climate crisis.

8.1. The Existing Environmental Chokepoints

Tourism, while an important global economic driver, has significant environmental implications. Hefty carbon footprints from airline travel, excessive demand for single-use plastic in hotels, overconsumption of resources like water and energy, and strain on local ecosystems from mass tourism all play a part in the climate conundrum. However, AI is evolving as a powerful tool to counteract these environmental chokepoints.

8.2. Introducing AI for Greener Practices

1. Machine Learning for Optimal Resource Use: Resource optimization is a key feature of sustainable tourism. Machine Learning (ML) algorithms, a subset of AI, can analyze historical consumption data of electricity, water, and other resources to predict future consumption patterns. Hotels can leverage these insights to reduce overuse and wastage.

2. AI for Better Waste Management: Waste generation is a significant environmental concern in the hospitality industry. Advanced AI-powered systems can sort and manage waste efficiently, leading to an effective reduction in landfill contributions.

3. Sustainable Travel Experiences: AI can promote eco-tourism by offering personalized trip recommendations that focus on nature preservation and low carbon footprints. This not only encourages responsible travel but also raises environmental awareness among tourists.

8.3. Deciphering the AI-Intervened Green Transition

Let's delve into the implications of these AI applications for sustainable tourism in the hospitality industry.

8.4. Resource Optimization: Cutting Costs and Carbon

Through the implementation of AI and machine learning, hotels can make accurate forecasts of resource requirements cutting unnecessary costs and reducing environmental impact. By way of illustration, suppose a hotel utilizes an ML algorithm to analyze the patterns of electricity usage in guest rooms. Over time, the system can identify peak usage hours and devise an optimal electricity usage schedule. Accordingly, air conditioning and lighting systems could automatically adjust to this schedule, using less power during off-peak times and reducing the hotel's overall electricity consumption.

8.5. Waste Management: A Smarter Approach

Use of AI in waste management can revolutionize the way hotels handle their hefty waste production. An example is AI-powered smart waste bins, which are capable of sorting waste for recycling purposes. These bins use sensors and cameras to identify the type of waste being disposed of, facilitating its appropriate segregation. This results in less waste winding up in landfills, optimizes recycling processes, and facilitates a more sustainable waste management approach in hotels.

8.6. Eco-Tourism: Personalized and Sustainable Travel Experiences

AI is instrumental in promoting sustainable travel practices. AI-powered platforms can offer eco-friendly travel suggestions to tourists based on their preferences. Imagine a travel recommendation engine that knows a user loves hiking. The system could recommend a variety of local hiking trails for the traveler to explore, thereby promoting local tourism and reducing carbon footprints, all while delivering a personalized eco-friendly experience.

8.7. Driving Sustainable Policies through AI

While these AI implementations promise a greener future, integrating them into strategy and policy is essential. Incorporating AI-driven sustainable practices in a hotel's brand ethos can not only improve its ecological footprint, but also strengthen customer loyalty, as more and more consumers are highlighting sustainability as a factor in their choice of service.

8.8. Case Studies: AI in Action

Herein, we'll review two cases that showcase the successful integration of AI within their sustainable practices:

1. Rainmaker's GuestREV: The hospitality revenue and profit optimization cloud service, GuestREV, uses AI to forecast demand and determine optimal room pricing. Its eco-consciousness reflects in its ability to optimize resource allocation.

2. Winnow Solutions: Winnow is using AI systems in commercial kitchens to monitor and minimize food waste by providing data-driven insights. The proprietary system captures and analyses waste data which then helps chefs make more informed decisions.

8.9. Conclusion: Shaping a Sustainable Future

The interplay of AI with the hospitality industry presents a unique opportunity to tackle tourism's environmental challenges. By fostering resource optimization, smarter waste management, and promoting eco-tourism, AI is not just empowering a more sustainable industry, but also echoing the urgency of climate action. As the industry continues to explore, adopt, and refine these AI-led innovations, the promise of a greener and more sustainable tourism industry looms closer than ever before.

Chapter 9. Challenges and Opportunities: Privacy Concerns and Ethical Dimensions of AI in Hospitality

Let's begin our examination at a point of growing concern in the realm of artificial intelligence – privacy and ethical dimensions. In the hospitality industry, with AI being employed to enhance guest experiences, streamline operations, and predict trends, the critical questions about data privacy and ethics have become focal points of discussion.

9.1. The Privacy Paradox

Firstly, to cater personalized experiences to guests, hospitality companies need to collect a large volume of data about them. This data often includes sensitive information such as personal preferences, credit card details, travel patterns, and even biometric data. The resulting paradox is that while customers want the personalized experiences that AI and big data can provide, they are also increasingly concerned about the privacy and security of their personal data.

The challenge here is to build robust and secure systems that can provide customized services without infringing on customer privacy. For instance, a hotel might use an AI-powered chatbot to offer personalized room service—but it's vital that all the information collected by the chatbot is secure and used only for the intended purpose.

Underpinning this challenge is the burgeoning range of global data protection laws like the EU's General Data Protection Regulation (GDPR) and the California Consumer Privacy Act (CCPA) in the U.S. Adherence to these regulations becomes an intricate task, impacting how AI tools can be developed and deployed. The risk becomes even more evident when data is shared with third-party entities, wherein companies lose control over how customer information is managed and secured.

9.2. The Paradox Solution: Transparent Data Practices

A potential solution to the privacy paradox lies in establishing transparent data practices. Hospitality companies can begin by openly stating their intentions and practices in relation to data collection, storage, usage, and sharing. Such transparency can earn customers' trust and foster more meaningful interactions. It's essential to remember that transparency includes not only informing customers but also giving them control over their data.

Another related approach is implementing privacy by design. This principle includes adopting measures to preserve privacy and meet regulatory demands beforehand in the design stage of any product or service. For instance, limiting the collection of data to only necessary information, securing collected data, anonymizing data as much as possible, and designing systems with data breaches in mind will prepare for worst-case scenarios.

9.3. Ethical Implications of AI

Next to the privacy concerns is the ethical dimension of AI in the hospitality industry. The question arises: how are decisions made and actions taken by AI tools evaluated from an ethical standpoint? AI algorithms are predominantly "black box" in nature, with decisions frequently made in ways that humans cannot interpret.

One pressing ethical challenge with AI is its potential propensity towards bias, often unconsciously programmed in by human developers or inherent in the data sets upon which AI algorithms are trained. This bias can be harmful, leading to prejudiced customer experiences or unequal employment practices.

Also, the increased use of AI may lead to reduced human interactions, thereby drastically changing the nature of hospitality, an industry that has traditionally been about personal touch and human connection.

9.4. Addressing Ethical Concerns

Addressing ethical concerns begins with creating and enforcing a robust ethical framework within the company. This framework should articulate the company's ethical stance and govern AI's responsible use. A good starting point might be to align AI practices with global standards such as the OECD Principles on AI.

Bias in AI can be tackled through careful audits of existing AI systems to detect and correct any inadvertent bias. At the same time, focusing on building diverse development teams and using diverse training data can help to avoid bias in future AI tools.

Companies should also carefully evaluate the AI-human balance in their processes. While AI can automate several tasks, the personal touch should not be completely omitted. The best experience often results from a delicate harmony where AI technology is used to enhance, not replace, human interaction.

9.5. Opportunities Amidst Challenges

The challenges associated with privacy and ethical dimensions of AI present an opportunity for hospitality companies to lead with responsibility, transparency, and inclusivity. A proactive approach to these concerns can differentiate a company in a crowded marketplace, demonstrating a genuine commitment to responsible AI usage.

Striking the right balance between delivering personalized AI-driven experiences and respecting privacy norms can launch a new era of trust and loyalty. Similarly, ethical AI practices can inspire admiration amongst guests, employees, and society at large, creating distinct value and competitive advantage.

As we dive deeper into the potentials of artificial intelligence, it is clear that the future of the hospitality industry will be shaped by those who can skillfully navigate these challenges and seize the opportunities they present. The path is complex, but the rewards are promising for those who dare to tread with mindful commitment to privacy, ethical decision making and customer experience.

Chapter 10. Case Studies: Noteworthy Implementations of AI in Global Hospitality Brands

Implementing AI-driven solutions in the hospitality sector isn't just a futuristic concept – it's happening right now. Major players in the industry are already utilizing AI to enhance customer experiences, streamline operations, and make strategic decisions. In this chapter, we will delve into a few real-world case studies that demonstrate these developments in action.

===AI at Hilton: Connie, the Robot Concierge

In 2016, Hilton Hotels, in collaboration with IBM Watson, introduced the first AI-enabled hotel concierge - 'Connie'. Connie lent her abilities to simplify hotel staff's workflow and personalize guest experiences.

Connie was designed to learn from human language, thus improving its recommendations over time. Guests could communicate with Connie using natural language, asking questions about hotel facilities, services, and local attractions. Connie's capability to 'learn' from these interactions enabled Hilton to gather valuable insights about what their guests value most, thereby tailoring the guest experience to meet and exceed those expectations. By supplementing human assistance with AI, Hilton combined the efficiency of technology with the warmth of personal interaction, creating a superior hospitality experience.

10.1. AI in Marriott: Chatbots and Room Customizations

Marriott has been embracing AI technology in several ways to enhance guest experience. One of these innovations is the Marriott's ChatBotlr. Introduced in 2017, this AI-based service assists guests with requests and queries, answering in real-time any questions about amenities, availability of services, and even local tourist spots.

Furthermore, Marriott Hotels have also used AI to create a personalized stay for each guest. Their partnership with Legrand and Samsung led to the creation of an Internet of Things (IoT) hotel room. These rooms, equipped with AI, allow guests to personalize their preferences such as setting the room temperature, lighting, or even choosing what content they want on their in-room TV. With time, these smart rooms learn and recall guests' preferences, creating a customized and comfortable stay for each guest.

10.2. Accor Hotels: Phil Welcome and AI-enhanced Accessibility

Accor Hotels offered a glimpse into the exciting potentials of AI in hospitality with the introduction of their robot staff member, Phil Welcome. Phil not only handles tasks such as informing guests about services and answering questions, but he can also detect and analyze guests' emotions through facial recognition, offering personalized interactions.

Taking AI implementation further, Accor has been pioneering in promoting accessibility features as well. They introduced Accor Key, which uses AI to enable keyless room entry, thus making for a seamless and contactless check-in experience for guests. AI-driven features like these contribute immensely, making the hospitality experience accessible to people with various physical capabilities.

10.3. InterContinental Hotels Group (IHG): AI for Revenue Management

While AI has significantly impacted customer-facing roles in hospitality, it's important to remember its equally crucial impact on the operational side. InterContinental Hotels Group (IHG) provides a perfect example with their Revenue Management System, equipped with machine learning algorithm.

This system gleans insights from historical booking data, market trends, and external factors like events and holidays, to predict demand and optimize room prices accordingly. As a result, it aids in driving profit by selling the right product to the right customer at the right time for the right price. This has shown how AI can transform decision-making in hospitality, shifting from a primarily intuition-based approach to a more data- and insight-driven one.

In conclusion, these case studies demonstrate how AI is transforming the landscape of the hospitality industry. They offer valuable lessons on how to utilize AI to enhance guest experiences, improve revenues, and make operations more efficient. As AI continues to evolve, it will be fascinating to see how new applications continue to shape this industry in unimagined ways.

Chapter 11. The Road Ahead: Future Trends of AI in Travel and Tourism

AI is destined to play a game-changing role in the tourism and hotel industry. As an emerging technology, it shall not only optimize various service operations through automation, intelligent algorithms, and automatic pattern recognition but also promises to provide seamless end-to-end experiences, making travel more personal, innovative, and enjoyable for customers.

11.1. Impact on Customer Services

AI's potential to revolutionize customer service is enormous. With the help of AI chatbots and virtual assistants, the hospitality industry can offer personalized 24/7 customer support, ensuring customers can find the answers they need, when they need them. AI-powered tools can analyze customers' needs, preferences, and questions quickly, offering personalized responses in real-time, thereby enhancing customer satisfaction and loyalty. It's certainly a tempo-setter for efficient and personalized interactions in the industry.

11.2. AI-Driven Personalization

The emphasis on travel personalization is ever-growing, as customers seek experiences tailored to their unique preferences. AI permits the customization of travel suggestions and offers based on individual's travel history and preferences through sophisticated algorithms and recommendation systems. Here, AI transforms into a technological concierge, suggesting personalized points of interest, dining venues or accommodations, all aimed at enhancing the user's overall experience.

11.3. Pricing and Revenue Management

AI's prowess extends to revenue management by predicting pricing trends. It helps organizations to understand and anticipate customer purchase behavior, allowing for dynamic pricing strategies in response to fluctuating demand. Machine Learning algorithms can mine historical data to identify demand patterns, providing insights into optimal pricing strategies for maximizing profitability.

11.4. Enhancing Travel with Augmented and Virtual Reality

Augmented and virtual reality (AR and VR), assisted by AI, are proving to be invaluable tools. They allow hotels, travel agencies, museums, and tourist attractions to provide virtual tours and previews. VR technology can simulate travel experiences, enabling customers to "try before they fly," while AR can transform on-ground experiences, providing interactive, contextually aware information to travelers in real-time.

11.5. Smart Rooms and IoT

The implementation of AI in the form of smart rooms and IoT in the hospitality sector represents the next step in the evolution of luxury and comfort. AI-powered smart rooms can automate room temperature, lighting, television, curtains, and much more, ensuring optimal comfort for guests. As a result, hotels can significantly elevate their customer service, offering an unparalleled and unique guest experience.

11.6. AI's Influence on Marketing Strategies

AI has a profound impact on marketing strategies within the travel and tourism sector. AI predictive analysis tools can analyze trends, track behavior, and understand user preferences. Travel businesses can tailor their marketing strategies accordingly, ensuring the right product or service is marketed to the right audience at the right time. The result? Higher conversion rates and a more compelling marketing strategy that resonates with customer needs.

11.7. Risk and Crisis Management

AI-driven tools can analyze vast amounts of data to predict potential risks, crises, or dilemmas in the travel and tourism industry. Tools such as AI-based early warning systems can foresee natural disasters, political unrest, or pandemic outbreaks that might affect travel plans. Such information helps businesses to proactively strategize, issue necessary advisories, and ensure the safety of travelers.

It's substantial to acknowledge that AI's role in the hospitality and travel industry is only at the dawn of its potential. The industry's foresight will determine its holistic incorporation, ensuring transparency, ethical norms, and data privacy are abided by. Incorporating AI promises exponential advancement – a peak into a future where AI doesn't eliminate the human touch, but instead magnifies and enhances the hospitality experience to unrivaled proportions. The road ahead is exciting, with endless explorations and opportunities for those ready to ride the tide of AI-enhanced travel and tourism. AI is more than just a technological wave; it's a catalyst for reshaping the travel and tourism industry.